i am Love

Denise,
I Love you! I
appreciate your spirit!

God bless!

i am Love

EVERY PIECE IS A CONTRIBUTION

J. E. GREEN

MORALS & VALUES PRESS

This is a work of nonfiction.
Nonetheless, names have been intentionally
omitted in order to conceal individuals' identities.

Copyright © 2017 by J. E. Green

Published in the United States by Morals & Values Press.

ISBN 978-0-9898501-6-2

To Love.

CONTENTS

INTRODUCTION

In 2011, the human development organization I was working for at the time was hired by the state of Louisiana's Office of Juvenile Justice also known as OJJ, to facilitate staff training. I was also asked to produce a symposium to tour OJJ's facilities and to develop a process by which I would have conversations with the young men there. The purpose of these conversations was to impress the importance of good decision making, the value of healthy relationships and to inspire the ambitious pursuit of a life of purpose.

Standing in the wide open space of the gymnasium at Bridge City Center for Youth, waiting for the one hundred plus young men to walk in, my eyes were fixed on the doors with great anticipation. Within the walls of that fortified building in Louisiana were young men who had barely lived their lives yet their decisions yielded long term consequences many of them were never ready to face. The weight of their criminal charges, unresolved experiences, and so much more was about to walk in to that room to meet me. I was interested in the so much more.

The door opened and chatter began to mount. As the young men filled in the bleachers, one by one I personally introduced myself and shook the hand of all but one. He refused to shake my hand, also expressing with more words than I will share, that I did not know him or where he was from. He went on to let me know with a few choice expletives that he would appreciate my immediate withdrawal from his personal space. Without hesitation, I continued to introduce myself to those I had not.

Over the hour that I spent speaking with those young men that day, we explored the many pieces of their lives. I shared with them many of my experiences growing up in the city of Baltimore, Maryland. Our similarities bridged our differences and ultimately created a space for understanding and inspired purpose. As I closed, I expressed to the group that I Loved them and that my Love for them and who they could become was authentic. I informed them that I could Love them because I had experienced the same Love from others who believed in me as I too believed in them. I encouraged them to supplement what they believed they wouldn't or couldn't be with that Love as I had in my youth and use it as a force to be and do better.

After I finished addressing the group, I had individual conversations with many of the young men. I shared my contact information with them. Then I prepared to leave as the young men exited the gym. However, I noticed the one young man who had refused to shake my hand was lingering behind. He walked up to me, offered a sincere apology and began to cry. He told me that no one had ever told him that they Loved him. I affirmed for him that I did. We spoke briefly about his life and agreed to keep in touch.

As a black man in America, unfortunately it's not uncommon to be associated with stories of incarceration. But my story is a unique one. By the age of twenty-three, I had spent over ten years of my life working in human development. My passion and ambition to see greatness actualized in the lives of others was established early on in life by virtue of the healthy relationships I had experienced in my youth. At age twelve I began traveling across the United States of America as a professional trainer, speaker and advocate, working with individuals and service providers seeking solutions for unresolved life experiences. Through that experience in Louisiana and many others I have come to understand that Love is powerful, yet often misunderstood. Our relationships and the experiences that they yield are embedded with unique obstacles that can lead to misunderstanding, pain, impatience and trauma. These are some of the obstacles that often skew our perception of Love. Without understanding, many of us become frustrated in our attempts to piece together the meaning of our experiences and make less than favorable decisions. However, if we remain open to the experiences Love continuously facilitates in our lives, Love has its own way of connecting our seemingly misshapen experiences, and ultimately creating clarity and insight into the purpose of our efforts in life and in Love.

Back at Bridge City, it was an *openness to Love* that created the opportunity for that young man and I to share a remarkable experience. It was the foundation for every experience thereafter when we spoke over the phone or through letters. That experience inspired him to change his life. He left that facility, got a job, and started a family. When we last spoke he was excited about all he plans to do in life for him and others. Considering the amazingly positive outcome of that experience, imagine the adverse affect had I responded in a less than Loving way.

Our experiences with Love are constantly shaping our lives as life and Love are inseparable. One Love experience at a time, the illustration of our life is perpetually developing from birth throughout our adult lives. By virtue of our thoughts we are consciously and unconsciously creators of our experiences. There is so much we gain in Love.

In 2012, while trying to make sense of pieces of my own life I was struggling to understand, I committed to being more open to Love. Over the course of two years I took time to seek resolution for the things I believed were unresolved in my past and present. With my intentionally developing consciousness I was able to witness many piece or experience joining one to another and those things that were once puzzling became these beautiful images of triumph in adversity.

i am Love is an outcome of that journey. Throughout this book I share my personal Love experiences with you because I believe the greatest way to evoke authentic Love is to share in honest self reflection. I hope that as you read and share in this experience of honest self reflection that you would be open to Love.

Love,

J

i am Love

CHAPTER ONE

COURTING

"Love demands that we gain perspective beyond perception."

It's interesting the amount of time we can spend getting to
know someone and still the possibility exists that we may
never come to completely understand who they truly are.
Drawing from a collection of experiences, both mine and
others, I've learned that it is highly probable to one day
wake up next to someone you've been in relationship with
for years, feeling as if you've awakened in the company of a
complete stranger. The same can even occur within the
relationship we sustain with the individual looking back at
us in the mirror.

In counsel and conversation, I often find that many people are unaware of who they truly are and uncertain as to how they have arrived at a particular place in their life. So easily we become distracted with the many things that intrigue us, only to look up and realize just how far away we are from what inspired us to begin the journey. Today, with a greater level of conciseness and clarity, I've come to know the importance of evaluating the many experiences life affords humanity through relationship. I believe the easiest way to determine exactly where a relationship diverts from its intended purpose is to locate the moment when Love is inadvertently exchanged in pursuit of selfish desire. A common example of this is the overtime spent at work and away from our Loved ones. Though our intention is not to deprive those we Love of our presence, our absence is also the absence of the present energy of our Love. Our absence creates the perception that our Love is also absent. This is important because many of us struggle to believe in a Love that we cannot see.

Love in its authentic form is an indescribable yet indisputable knowing that radiates from within and permeates all aspects of our lives. Love is not blind as some would have us to think. In Love we are able to clearly identify the object of our Love and how it came to be. Be it Love of one self, Love of another human being, or the Love that one may feel toward something they are passionate about. Love demands that we gain perspective beyond perception. It asks how, rather than why. And at the core of how we Love is the key to discerning if reciprocity exist within the experience.

The *why* behind human behavior can and often does change. The reasons why we choose to enter into a particular relationship today may be the very reasons that, that relationship ends six to nine months later. You may like that he's a spur of the moment kind of guy or that she's a free spirited woman, until you realize he is also that way with his money; and that she is so free spirited that she would rather not be tied down to just one person. In addition to our varying approaches to relationships, our emotions tend to bring out the worst in us in our desire to know *why*. We can become impatient, irrational and even worse, impressionable. We may be easily swayed by things that arouse us but never quite take us to the peak of our purpose in relationship.

Asking *how,* immediately demands a plan of action and more readily exposes competency or the ability to carry out a communicated plan successfully. When we ask *how*, we remove emotion and get right to accountability. Feelings are fickle and accountable to no one. But communicated intentions can be verified by actions that prove them to be true. When people abandon their communicated intentions in relationships, they let us know their Love has changed. Then it's on us to make a conscious decision concerning the value of our own Love.

The purpose of every relationship, *what* we're in it for, should always be Love. I believe at the nucleus of human life there is only Love. And as we evolve in our thinking we can choose to be conscious of and create from our nucleus moment by moment. Or we can live solely based upon perceptions. As perception is most readily formed by trying to resolve new occurrences with past experiences, this can create an inability to acknowledge Love's presence when we would benefit from Love's presence the most, when it does not look or feel as it has at any point before. The relationships that demand that we give more than we have before, and see things in a way we've never had to, tend to teach us the most about ourselves. It's our choice to be engaged in those relationships that ultimately builds character and our consciousness of Love and life.

Every decision we make alters our position in Love, as no two moments in life are the same. This means each moment and each decision connected to that moment demands that we have an adequate plan of action to gain perspective, otherwise failure is almost certain. In understanding and accepting this way of thinking we can eliminate the desire to continually ask, *why*?

In my teenage years, I had a way with words that helped me to win the affection of young women. With poetic rhythms and R&B songs, I could mask the fact that my interests were often self-serving. If I would tell a young lady I liked her, she would always ask, "why?" My reply would often be a generic answer used before, such as, "your smile, your personality, the way you carry yourself."Or I'd even say, "There is just something about you that intrigues me." I knew that by creating a perception that everything about me was kin to their feelings of relationship, I could use those feelings to manipulate the relationship for my own interest.

Those brief interactions usually ended with the young lady hurt and me on to the next self-indulgent conquest to prove my masculinity. It's not that I didn't desire Love, rather that my past experiences, much like theirs, had given me a faint perception and no real perspective of how to Love. At that age, though I couldn't describe "what" Love was, I had a feeling, as we all innately do. But Love is only truly understood by practical application.

It therefore took a rather unsuspecting young lady to introduce me to Love. We met in the hallway of what is now my high school alma mater, Mergenthaler Vocational Technical High school in Baltimore, Maryland – also known as MERVO. She was walking one way down the hall and I the other; she smiles, I smile and we kept walking. About ten minutes later as I was walking down the hallway of an entirely different floor, the same young lady comes walking from the opposite direction. This time I smile, she smiles, and I say, "Are you stalking me?" She says, "Umm, I think it's you who's stalking me." We laughed and kept walking, disappearing at opposite corners. Though that was our very first encounter, it wouldn't be the last. Every day until I graduated, I saw her in the hall and we'd smile, speak and keep walking. Our innocent exchange faded in to seemingly nothing.

The summer after I graduated, I passed on the opportunity to audition for a performing arts school in Los Angeles, California, which was a decision that completely contradicted the seven years of my life I spent in musical theater. However, convinced that it was too far from home, I chose to stay and work that summer at a local restaurant. The following year, I registered to attend an in-state university. I remember right before the semester began, my mom, my godfather and I loaded a few items into his Toyota Highlander and drove down to Princess Anne, Maryland for orientation at the University of Maryland Eastern Shore. I had enrolled as a sociology and social work major.

Before I knew it, my first semester was over and I was headed home on break. One day, while logged into MySpace, I came across the profile of the girl with the smile that I had seen in the hallway. I sent her a friend request and after we exchanged several messages, I found out that she was currently staying on campus for a required summer program at the same in-state university I was attending. We began making plans to hang out that coming semester when we returned to school.

Once arriving back at school, we eventually ran into one another, caught up for a bit, and then went our separate ways. At first, we didn't spend much time together. Then, periodically, we began to meet up between classes to just sit and talk. It didn't take long for us to start spending most of our days together. We'd go to lunch together, basketball games, and sit outside on campus all night with some mutual friends.

After sometime passed, it became apparent that we were both interested in being more than just friends. I was operating out of my normal bag of tricks, working my repertoire of poems and R&B songs. But she wasn't concerned with those things. She'd often come over to my house, I'd make subtle advances, and she'd deny each one. But one night after a couple months had passed, she finally gave in to what we both knew had become inevitable.

A couple days later, as we lay in the bed watching TV, I remember her turning to me and asking, "What is this going to be?" I was immediately thrust into an internal meltdown. I never thought that far into the situation. I was content without labeling what it was because of the fringe benefits. But at that moment I knew, without my consent, she had made up in her mind what she wanted before she even asked the question. It was evident in her tone and posture. Just like that the tables turned and I was now focusing on the *Why*. Why now? Why me? ...Why not?

Maybe it was Karma. Maybe it was something else. Either way, her question and her approach to courting forced me to decide if I was going to be a willing participant. At eighteen years old, I was not fully present enough to realize the impact of my decision. I couldn't conceive that my next words would be the very key that would unlock a five year relationship that would completely alter the trajectory of my life and be an essential part of the development of my perspective of Love.

Truthfully, I had reservations about pursuing anything more than a friendship (with the possibility of continued benefits) with this young lady. She was and still is a beautiful soul; however, our thought processes were very different. I have a propensity to analyze and even over analyze, for the sake of not wanting to miss a detail in the process. In comparison, she preferred to make up her mind about a thing and just do it.

Both styles arguably have their benefits. But together, in our specific case, they produced a very potent cocktail of conflicting thoughts fueled by the perceptual *why* thought process. I now know that the demise of our relationship came at the proverbial hands of *why*. Why do I have to explain this? Why doesn't it make sense to you? Why can't we just be on the same page?

At times, my "why desire" pushed so forcefully for the satisfaction of my individual wants that it drove us apart. The "why desire" is again our attempt to justify a specific person, place, or thing in our lives by our past, in an effort to gain contentment. The *why desire* is completely about satisfying our emotional being. But our emotions can be extremely messy when we have yet to conceptualize that emotions are essentially chemical reactions taking place in our mind brought on via the experiences we have through our five senses. They can be managed if we make the effort to. While courting, if we are solely driven by our emotions, we place restrictions on the possibilities that exist within the many relationships we will encounter over our life time.

I chose to use my past relationship as an example because I believe it is the most common area of understanding for most people. The relationship we have with our significant other is often the greatest source of present energy in our life. Good or bad, we tend to take that energy with us everywhere we go. We all can identify with a time we've had to end a romantic relationship because the energy was so toxic, we couldn't figure out why we were there anymore. But the "why desire" is not only limited to our intimate relationships with our life partners. It often exists in our careers as well.

For instance, if we invest our time and emotion into a job without receiving what we believe is adequate recognition, or are passed over for a promotion, the feeling of rejection can drive our desire to know why so much, that we become emotionally attached to the rejection giving it roots in our career aspirations. We may stop applying to new positions, and when we see others promoted around us, we may hold discouraging feelings. Even as a ministry worker in my former church, I can personally attest to the feeling of rejection while working in ministry.

No matter the place, it never feels good to be misunderstood, or to feel as if the person, job or thing you Love and give your time to leaves you unfulfilled. It's necessary to constantly remind ourselves that we must be driven by Love rather than our emotions. In doing so we are able to realize the adequate and appropriate amount of energy necessary to establish peace regardless of our circumstance.

Creating our lives with Love at our core ultimately produces the best possible outcome in all areas of our lives. Love gives us the ability to be truly happy because it is rooted in gratitude. Gratitude teaches us that the value of happiness exists within us and not in our pursuit of things. It's not until we decide to be and do what we Love that we begin to experience true happiness in our relationships, careers, and in everything else we chose to do. This is not to be confused with the often short lived, Loving me first mantra some adopt after an unfavorable outcome in a relationship. That can evoke pseudo happiness, inflate the ego, and make people oblivious to the reality that the world does not revolve around one individual human being's inability to be vulnerable.

That person inhibits happiness from entering their atmosphere by shutting off their ability to compassionately partake of others' Love experiences. It's a very lonely way to live. In contrast, when we choose Love as a guiding principle, commit to nurturing our level of consciousness about Love and practically apply what we know to our everyday lives, happiness shows up in everything.

The way we court life is the way we court Love and vice versa. To be incomplete in one is to be incomplete in the other. The only way to truly know ourselves is to fervently seek to know the presence of Love in us and Love's presence in the people and things we are truly passionate about. If you want to eliminate confusion in your life, only court the things you find Love in. If you want to avoid wasting time on people who may break your heart, dead end jobs that drain you, non-reciprocal friendships, seek to court the Love within those people, places and things that reflect the same Love that exist within you.

While we are all individually journeying to know Love, we are simultaneously engaging in relationship with the universe. If we don't strategically agree about how we arrive at Love, then those connections are more of a hindrance than of benefit to us. Regardless of one's given intentions, true motives become apparent in the process. If the process does not match one's given intention it's much easier to make a sound decision as to whether or not the Love we need exist within that relationship. With this understanding now we are able to know Love, court Love and give Love.

CHAPTER TWO

THE DECISION

"One thought has the influence to change the trajectory of our entire life."

As previously mentioned, there in my college apartment lying in the bed with a beautiful young lady whom I had grown fond of over the past few months, I was contemplating *the decision* to further our mutual friendship with benefits. I must admit the circumstances of the moment didn't help foster authenticity in my decision making process. Nevertheless, my reservations withstanding, my reply to her question was, "Whatever you want it to be."

I know now what an awful answer that was. That day, *the decision* to utter those words appeared to be one of the least impactful decisions I'd ever make. But that decision, as I stated earlier, became the beginning of a huge shift in my life and in my relationship with Love.

At that time, I would never have fathomed that a few seemingly chance encounters in the hallway of my old high school would lead to that moment; or, any of the moments that would follow. I knew I was making a commitment, but to what? I had no clue. In my mind, I thought that *the decision* I was making was a righteous one. For the first time, I was going to care for someone else more than I cared about my own selfish desires. As my decision was taking shape, we had the chance to share more about our upbringing. And while it continued to be very clear that our lives were very different, we bonded over a desire for authentic relationship. Reluctantly though, I resolved within myself that I was able to give her something I assumed she desperately needed.

To be completely transparent, I convinced myself that I was going to save her. I convinced myself that I was rescuing her from the very vivid portrait of chaos she had painted throughout our many conversations. She needed to experience being Loved. And I was just the person to give her that Love. What I did not realize was that I had yet to find out for myself what Love was, what it required, and most of all, the consequences that arise as a result of pursuing Love.

What was unknown then over time has undoubtedly has revealed itself. Today, I believe life is a collection of moments. Each of those moments is produced by the energy facilitated by thought. Every thought is significant, so significant, that one specific thought has the influence to change the trajectory of our entire life. Ultimately, that's what this relationship did for me.

Every day we awake, often living out a routine that we have established overtime. There are things we do every day that don't take much thought at all. They are moments we've likely lived before, so we do them naturally. But when an unpredictable force or energy infringes upon that routine, it can alter our entire day.

A good example would be encountering a bad car accident on the drive into work. As traffic slows, your thought process immediately shifts. You may begin to focus on the list of to do's you're already behind on, and as time ticks by, you become impatient. It's also possible the opposite can happen. It's possible that compassion takes over, gratitude settles in, and in that moment you realize just how precious life is. The process may differ depending upon the individual. However, what we all share is the experience of present energy, by way of thought, constantly changing our lives.

The same can also be said about lack of present energy. There are certain things we grow accustomed to that signal or confirm significant moments of our life. A text or call to say good morning reassures us that we are on someone's mind, and we sustain happiness for another fifteen minutes. The alarm clock waking us up, if we don't hit snooze, assures that we make it to work on time and we get paid. But when the alarm doesn't sound, we over sleep and we are late for work. If we lose a significant relationship, the good morning texts stop and something that seems so simple has a monumental impact.

In both situations, the absence of a specific presence can leave a life altering void in a moment that otherwise might truly benefit from present energy. When the alarm clock doesn't sound or when the voice of a lost Love no longer breaks through the silence of our lives, triggering certain awareness, it alters moments that were once warmly familiar into moments of anxiety or frustration. And as our thought processes shifts, the energy produced as a result is perpetually transforming our lives. The present energy our thoughts produce, encountering our everyday circumstances, is establishing our existence over the span of a lifetime.

To be conscious of this universal truth affords us the opportunity to create our lives inside of the moment that was produced for us to create. Otherwise we may find ourselves overwhelmed with energy established by the actions or inaction of others, the presence or absence of familiar energy.

In chapter one, I shared my personal belief that at the nucleus of human life there is only Love. When we choose to create from Love, the energy we produce is Love. Our thoughts of Love converted into energy by our will to act on our thoughts, produces a present energy of Love. That in turn initiates a shift, inevitably transforming our entire lives. All of this takes place in a seemingly simple but highly intricate moment. Each moment linked to the next, through the momentum created by energy acting on thought, ultimately becomes the story of our evolution, or legacy as I like to call it.

There are two other major components to mastering *the decision*. The first is to understand momentum and how it affects our ability to make decisions. The second is to know the truth about one's will and knowing how to enfranchise your will with Love.

Webster's Dictionary defines momentum as the force or strength something has when moving. Most often momentum is purely associated with a physical object, but I encourage you to also consider momentum as the force that carries us from thought to thought. Scientifically, the momentum ($p=mv$) of a physical object is determined by multiplying its mass (m) by its velocity (v). However, the momentum of a particular thought in our lives' is determined by multiplying tolerance (t) by will (w) or $p=tw$.

I believe tolerance is determined by two factors: DNA and experience. The first, is DNA, or in short, the things that we inherit from our ancestry. These things are both biological and psychological. It's important to know what we have inherited because it gives us a foundation of understanding. During the years that I've worked with young people, it's often physically and emotionally apparent which young people have little or no relationship with a parental figure by their behaviors and even their willingness to be a follower of what others around them are doing in an effort to belong to something. Those same behaviors can follow us into adulthood. Though we can't change our inheritance, we can adjust our behavior to establish an alternate foundation that will help us to succeed in life and in Love.

The second factor of tolerance is experience. Often, we attempt to measure current or future experiences against past experiences. Though this behavior would be viewed as normal by many, I would argue that it can be a hindrance in determining one's true depth of experience. A series of bad experiences can be quite discouraging and sway our tolerance, possibly leaving us closed off. I wholeheartedly believe our experiences all come to contribute a piece of understanding to the purpose of our existence. Seemingly small or large in relevance, each experience is significant, just as the thought and energy produced as an outcome of that experience is equally significant.

Our tolerance of a thing or thought determines whether we accept or reject it. At first glance, the depth of this statement is not truly visible. But considering we choose to acknowledge the presence of a thing or thought by whether or not we accept it, we have to consider that tolerance then takes on a new meaning.

For example, The Civil Rights Movement for some "was" a long and hard fought effort to improve the conditions of Blacks living in the United States of America. To others the movement to advance the conditions of Blacks in American is as relevant today as it has ever been. Still, there are also some who denied the presence of inequity then, as there are those who deny it to this day, all believing their way, their cause, to be just. But if any cause lacks tolerance, it not a cause at all but rather a reaction to one's own will. It is an inability to be tolerant. The same exists in Love. When we lack tolerance for Love, we lack the ability to authentically acknowledge its presence. And if Love is the nucleus of life and we can't acknowledge it, we are left with a fear of a present energy we don't understand.

One of the biggest contributors to inadequate or inhibited tolerance is the inability to process pain properly. Pain through evolution has become one of life's most profound teachers. However, it is not meant to be feared but rather understood. If we understand what brings us pain, we can then make an intelligent decision whether or not to tolerate it. I say whether or not because sometimes Love requires suffering. However, that's another chapter. We'll get to that later.

Now, with a general understanding of tolerance, the second component of momentum comes into play. This component is will. After I have determined whether or not to tolerate a thing, now my will dictates the extent of that thing's ability to be present in my life. Our will is how we chose to invest our energy in a particular person, place, or thing. Not to be confused with desire, will is a conscious effort to carry out a decision after it has been made. Desire is an innate or influenced attraction to a person, place, or thing. Will requires focus while desire can operate purely off of fixation. Will is more deliberate; and without consistent exercise, one's will can and will diminish.

Tolerance multiplied by will determines the momentum of a thought carried out in our lives. Thoughts of success can motivate one to achieve and overcome the many obstacles that may lie in the way of that success. Thoughts of sadness can stagnate progress and even lead to depression and a perpetual state of fear. I've had the opportunity to experience both ends of the spectrum while learning a great deal about myself. One of the most important things I learned is that depression is not for me.

This formula, tolerance x will = momentum, established an awareness of what influences my thoughts. I now know when I'm making a decision from a place of Love or a place of fear, and I can change or alter my thought to align with

my purpose. In as much as this is still a truth I am daily
becoming one with, it's a truth I intend to pursue for life.

An idea driven by purpose is undeniable because it thrives
only on its will to live out its purpose. That day in my
campus apartment, *the decision* I was making wasn't just
about a relationship with another human being. But it was
a decision to enter into a relationship with Love itself.
Every time we enter into any relationship with a person,
place, or thing, unbeknownst to us, we ultimately choose to
enter into a more depth relationship with Love. The
experiences that we take on are to further our knowing
about our self and about Love. We must be courageous.
We have to be firm in our beliefs. And most importantly
we need to be reverent of Love in every moment. It's not
always easy, but I find peace in knowing that Love is
always present.

Just as the sun is always lighting the sky, so is Love in our
lives. However, night or fear, can at times cast a shadow
over our life, giving the illusion that Love has gone away.
But even in the night, as the moon sits amongst the stars
reflecting the sun's light from the other side of the world, so
does the light exist within us all to illuminate our darkest
days.

Metaphorically, tolerance allows us to acknowledge the
night but not let it consume us. Our will then focuses on the
moon knowing that it is the reflection of the sun. Our
momentum carries us through to the next thought, the next

moment and the next day, on to evolution and legacy. For so many reasons we are not always conscious of this process. But this concept applied to Love unlocks an unlimited wealth of power to free ourselves from depression or a legacy of poor decisions and unhealthy relationship.

Knowing this, every day I choose Love.

CHAPTER THREE

MOVING IN

"Our movement, directly or indirectly, impacts every one of our relationships."

After two majors and a year of the collegiate experience on the Eastern Shore, I was ready to leave. It was never my innate desire to go to a four year college. But I certainly acknowledge that attending the University of Maryland Eastern Shore, was a significant personal experience for me. When it was all said and done, I desired to pursue life on my own terms and prepared myself to live with the consequences.

My grandmother's passing in 2007 also contributed to my early exit from college. After all it was a conversation I had with her that ultimately solidified my decision to attend school in the first place. My grandmother was the epitome of 1Corinthians 13. She was patient and kind, never envious, boastful or prideful. She was a woman of honor, selflessness, not easily angered and quick to forgive. She protected her family, trusted in those who others wouldn't, and hoped for those who had none. She not only persevered but created a way for others to as well. Carole "Polly" Green never failed me and as far as I know, she was the only person in my lifetime that never lied to me.

The loss of such a significant truth changed me. After her death, I felt there were very few truths left to believe in. College, for me, was not one of them. In my second semester, I spent a lot of days in my apartment writing. Writing has always been one of my greatest truths. It's a gift I inherited from my mother. Music is gift I inherited from my father. No matter what, I can always find peace in music. Combining the two: songwriting became a new truth. I obsessed over it.

I vividly remember the day I received a call from a hometown friend, with whom I would collaborate with on the weekends when I was home from school. This particular day he was in New York with a Baltimore record label to meet a very accomplished music producer. My friend called to ask if I could hop on a plane that day and come to New York. The producer was impressed with the label's rapper, who the meeting was initially for, but he was really looking for a singer.

As a first year college student without a job, I had no way to make it from Princess Anne, Maryland to New York City. Missing that opportunity further fueled my desire to leave school and when the semester ended I went home and moved back in with my mom. I got a job but continued to focus on my music. I'd work during the day and spend every night at the studio writing and recording for myself and other artists.

Post "the decision," my girlfriend and I continued our long distance relationship through the following semester. She and I were almost inseparable. Every weekend she'd come home from school and we would spend every possible moment together. She would eventually transfer back home to Baltimore and pursue a degree in nursing at a local university. Prior to her move back home, I had already contemplated moving out on my own. But our conversation, once she returned home, progressed to a discussion of us moving in together. At 19 and 18, both of our parents had their reservations, but after many long conversations, our determination outweighed their reservations and we began our search for a place.

Our criteria for living standards were pretty simple. The place had to be affordable. We found a one bedroom, one bathroom apartment at a community called White Springs, which is located in Baltimore County. I can recall our excitement on the day we signed our lease. We got the keys, and that first night we stayed in our new place with nothing but a pallet we made on the floor. The pallet was comprised of a few comforters and the pillows taken from my room at my mother's house.

Neither of us owned much. We were so focused on the belief in Love we had for one another that what we lacked didn't seem to matter. My last day at my mother's house, I remember packing my car and leaving West Baltimore. The drive to Nottingham, Maryland was somewhat symbolic of the transition taking place in my life. I was leaving a familiar place headed to a new experience, in an unfamiliar environment.

For most of us, when we consider moving, generally we tend to consider what kind of environment we would like to be in. We prefer a clean neighborhood, with an esthetically pleasing landscape. New places should look and smell new, all of the appliances need to function properly and more than anything we hope our neighbors will be of like mind. At the very least, we'll be content with respectful neighbors that steer clear of our space. Most often we begin our search with a checklist of must-haves. But rarely are all the items on our list available.

We start out firm without room for compromise on our ideals. Yet reality tends to conflict with our list. We're ultimately forced to discern our wants from our needs. And we have to decide if we are searching for a place that suits our lifestyle today or our plans for the future. Decisions made solely for today's lifestyle tends to be short lived. As life changes so can our heart for our current location. When searching for residence that coincides with our future plans, we strategically take potential growth and transitions into account. It's the difference between purchasing and renting. Regardless of our choice to rent or purchase, moving still takes effort.

Life often demands that we move. When we don't meet life's demands we forfeit our ability to positively impact the "gray matter" moments of life. The moments before complacency, fear, or procrastination lead to periods of stagnation. We become stagnant when moving appears to require an effort we are either incapable of producing or not willing to put forth. The inability to appropriately and adequately engage life, results in life happening to us rather than for us. In this moment, life seemingly becomes a curse. Further inaction leads to an uncontrollable spiral of blame, perpetually fueled by self-serving misperceptions.

The energy produced as a result of our decisions is shaping our lives, directly and indirectly impacting every possible relationship we have and will ever establish. Our moving, in every moment is such an integral part of how that energy is shared.

Renters are not usually obligated to consider value when moving because renting is typically a temporary concept. Nor does the individual with temporary intentions in a relationship take into account another's human capital. The wise investor not only considers the value of a potential asset, they anticipate the value of their investment to grow exponentially overtime. To see that growth actualized, the wise investor will deliberately seek ways to increase the value of their asset.

I am not and never have been a licensed financial advisor. But during my time in banking, I was able to see how so many of the commonsense practices and strategies so easily translate to moves we make in relationships. I quickly learned the value of investing and ownership. While ownership certainly takes tremendous effort, the equity you gain increases your net worth. Only ownership equates to equity. And while investing requires taking risk, the only way to yield a good return is to be vested in something good for your future. Even while losses are technically inevitable, if managed properly, you may recover your losses and still see an increase on the upturn of a new era.

We invest to improve our position in life just as we do in Love.

People often say location is everything. But even after we've found an ideal location we still have to move in. Moving in, or the act of deliberately transferring things from one environment to another, requires both effort and considerable thought. If you care to be efficient, one might ponder what to bring and what to discard. You may even consider placing some things in storage while deciding exactly what to do with them?

In relationships, it's one thing to bring furniture, or a television, but moving the sum of your life experiences, thoughts, and energy into one shared environment requires a different kind of effort. Though the same concept of efficiency should apply, admittedly I've personally experienced relationships in which considerable thought never took place before physically or figuratively moving in all of the stuff. Initially, it can appear that everyone has brought every great thing about themselves to the relationship. Despite the small things, like the noises people make while eating and strands of hair left on the bathroom sink, relationships are initially magical. We find a way to rationalize away the things that bother us because we believe this "one" is the one.

Even in the bliss of a new relationship, each person's traumatic life experiences or TLEs still must be accounted for prior to moving in. If not, TLEs will gradually reveal themselves, because all traumatic life experiences inevitably do. Some signs of traumatic life experiences that appear in relationship can be managed through compassionate conversation and a plan of action rooted in compromise. Other TLEs may require group, couples, or individual therapy facilitated by a licensed professional. Conflicts stemming from unresolved TLEs can create a contentious and highly unpredictable environment.

Many relationships have a metaphoric to-do list of unresolved TLEs without any urgency to confront and resolve them. Abuse, molestation, rape, neglect, poverty, homelessness, addiction, mental disorders, sexuality, spirituality, fiscal irresponsibility, illiteracy and trust are a few unspoken pains and insecurities we can unconsciously bring and unpack in every relationship we commit ourselves to. Privately and publicly, intimate, work, and spiritual relationships are all affected by our ability to adequately determine the impact of TLEs in our life.

Promising relationships that could improve the lives of its participants and the environment around them are at times doomed from the very beginning when one or both parties aren't mindful to take the time to give considerable thought about the impact of their life experiences. If we want a healthy relationship, we should be honest about what fears those experiences have birthed. In doing so we give our partners a chance to authentically support us where we are stagnant. These are areas of opportunity. Working together to overcome TLEs in an environment of authentic Love builds resilience and trust in the individual and strengthens the bond of relationship simultaneously. This also lays the foundation for acts of Love that consistently reaffirm the purpose of us committing to a relationship.

A healthy relationship is an environment in which we should also be afforded the opportunity to share the strengths we've cultivated through our life's experiences. We should be unselfish, yet still conscious and compassionate to the communication styles of others in sharing our strengths. Our strengths should be of value to our partners and our partner's strengths should be of values to us. Most importantly, we should collectively seek to further strengthen our relationship by building on the strengths we've been fortunate enough to cultivate already. Complacency breeds discord and we should always be seeking to be better for ourselves and within our relationships.

Knowing and sharing our strengths and areas of opportunity does not totally eliminate the fact that there will always be some things that are unknown or unrealized. Sharing what we don't know is a true test of humility in relationship. Uninhibited, compassionate sharing diminishes the presence of fear, judgment, the false perception of perfection, and simultaneously advocates for authenticity.

Every moment is an opportunity for us to increase our long-term gain by increasing our long- term investment. Relationships are equitable and inequitable. Inequitable relationships provide temporary satisfaction. They are self-focused, fragile when faced with adversity of any kind, and hinge on its participant's ability to tolerate the things they don't like or understand about each other. Equitable relationships are established overtime as we surrender all of ourselves to Love in every facet of our lives over a lifetime. Equitable relationships demand a long-term investment strategy comprised of patience, long suffering, forgiveness, humility, compassion and most importantly inclusiveness.

The best day of living in that one bedroom one bathroom apartment at White Springs was the day we unpacked our things to put everything where it belonged. Selflessly and respectfully we handled each other's things, affirming one another in our decisions, compromising as needed and repeatedly acting on our commitment with small but consistent gestures of our Love. We brought all we had and we unpacked it together, in preparation of sharing a living space. Likewise, our preparation and plan of action for moving in life and Love must be both physical as well as psychological. When you think about it, it makes no sense at all to ever consider moving all our life experiences, thoughts, and energy into one shared environment with other human beings, only to create barriers of separation that inhibit the progression of Love within the opportunity time has afforded us.

Admittedly, I was just as unprepared moving into that one bedroom apartment as I was making *the decision* I made in college. Ignorance is blissful, until Love makes it awkwardly apparent that it does not play second fiddle in anyone's band of bad decisions. Love will not shrink itself to accommodate our unresolved experiences. It will not tolerate our moving in things, people and places that don't accompany our purpose. While what we bring to a relationship certainly has significance, it's not what we bring that's most important. Each of us has a responsibility to monitor, manage and maintenance the shared energy of our relationships in a way that make us credible, honest, accountability partners. Otherwise we're just moving in to fall out.

CHAPTER FOUR

FALLING OUT

*"At times, Love requires for us to build blindly from a memory
that has yet to take place in the earth."*

My first and last attempt at being someone's savior ended
horribly. There was yelling. There was cursing. There was
blame without real admission of wrong doing. I was
nothing like the "Nazarene" many have come to know and
Love. But I was earnest in my ambitions to fall in Love.

"Falling in Love" is typically how we describe the
maturation of a new relationship. Yet falling seems to
better describe what happens when known intentions in
Love become unclear or blurred. When something bursts
our bubble of perceived perfection, over time we may find
ourselves plummeting into the reality that the relationship
may not work. Heavy with the weight of so many

emotions, we experience frustration, doubt, indecision, and fear, as we approach our deciding moment. In an instant, the gravity of your circumstance brings you to an undeniable, uncomfortable truth and all you can do is brace for impact.

Out of respect for the privacy of the other person in that relationship, I won't go into exact specifics of the falling out. It all began with unresolved frustrations, frustration I caused often by being egotistical and frustration I experienced as a result of our dissenting life experiences.

Frustration starts off quite innocent. Small annoyances that you were able to accept at the inception of the relationship begin to feel like dull nudges to your equilibrium. To avoid confrontation, we typically address things in a lighthearted, almost joking manner. While behind the disingenuous smile that accompanies our words, a starch truth rises. We may say, "Babe, stop." But the authentic translation is, "I hate that and I wish that you would never ever do it again." But by the time we realize the small annoyance is so much more, it has already become a developed habit.

Now that dull nudge is like a pimple. It's there. You see it, feel it. You want it to go away. You want to burst it so bad, but if you do it may leave a scar. You analyze the annoyance, trying to determine the right time and approach to dealing with it. Your patience is running low. And though your tolerance has somewhat diminished you still care enough about the outcome of the relationship that you want to mitigate the outcome as much as possible. This stage of frustration may result in a more serious conversation that you hope will go well and bring clarity and resolution to the issue.

However, sometimes these things escalate to a status reminiscent of a rash. You do all you can not to scratch it, but it still itches. And ironically it seems satisfaction only comes when you scratch. But when you do, it only becomes inflamed and maybe even worse than it was initially. At this point, you've got to apply some sort of treatment because the conversing doesn't work the way it used to. You may decide to talk to someone who will listen and hopefully they will provide some good insight, something you haven't tried yet to treat the issues in your relationship.

This moment is pivotal because it is a nonrefundable investment, drawn directly from the bank of trust you've established over the extent of your relationship. Placing your trust in the hands of a successful advisor, someone with proven relationship experience, should yield a return of clarity, maybe even hope for the relationship. For the sake of comfort or because of fear, some people choose to talk to close friends of relatives about their relationship. But know because someone knows you, it doesn't make them an expert advisor to your situation. In fact, it may foster biased advice making you appear better off than you actually are.

Titles withstanding, it's imperative that we share the right thing with the right person, to receive the right feedback for our circumstance. Sharing your business with people who are eager to know the frustrations of your relationship is like investing your trust into a Ponzi scheme. Those people are in the business of self-satisfaction, not your well-being. Such experiences can further your frustration and leave you looking for answers to question you didn't have before. You'll know you've spoken with a good advisor when the interaction produces a plan and the tools necessary to carry out that plan. The greatest intention remains just a thought without the proper tools to accomplish the task at hand. Know your audience because trust is a currency no one can afford to squander.

Beyond frustration, we often face doubt. Doubt is the pessimistic spirit that surfaces whenever we are uncertain of what we deserve. Doubt can only exist in a space that faith has willingly vacated. And until you identify and seal the void in your life where doubt has now gained access, it will continue to attack your faith in all things, self included. Initially, doubt is subtle, but its persistent nature, overtime, can forge its way through your lives, paralyzing faith, rendering it seemingly useless. This is most often recognizable in people who possess great potential in Love but are unable to operate beyond inconclusive thought. Or simply put, it's a glass half empty, never half full mentality.

Doubt is never far behind the evidence of something great. It is parasitic in its ability to sift purpose from all things meaningful in our journey to know Love. Doubt has no need to linger in the presence of defeat, nor will it. Once it has sifted every ounce of purpose from you, a cognitive shift takes place and you begin to consciously avoid the principles that first guided you. Hope can appear to be unreal, and you may willingly go through life void of Love and true purpose, seeking happiness in the accumulation of things for the sake of checking boxes on society's list of must-haves.

Many of us experience doubt in our careers as we navigate our way to success. It may be a new opportunity at work or a career we've been actively seeking for some time; adjusting to change often brings about doubt because change directly impacts our faith. Anyone who's ever experienced working in an environment that contradicts what your skills and efforts deserve has had to make a faith dependent decision to move on to something better. We all want the greatest possible experiences and the greatest possible outcome for ourselves. However, doubt is never far behind the greatness we seek to experience.

The presence of doubt causes you to consider why you might not attain what you know you deserve. While some will immediately give way to that doubt, others push forward to overcome it. Though things may not be exactly as you would like, being faithful to seeking your best possible self eventually affirms what is purposed for your life. Your faith in action delivers the things you seek in purpose. Striving to maintain relationships in which you "sort of see" how it "may align" with aspirations you "could eventually" come to Love is a slippery slope. With considerable thought, the intelligent being aspires only to things that are purposed and purposeful.

The relationships that are purposed for your life transcend instant gratification. They aren't the relationships that appease your current fears or satisfy a niche emotional state you've deemed safe. They require you to be both bold and mindful simultaneously. Greatness requires relentless faith in ourselves and faith in those with whom we must relate. At times, Love requires for us to build blindly from a memory that has yet to take place in the earth.

Faith is a radical idea to those who lack faith. But for those who believe in a purposed life for themselves, faith is a tool of discernment used when our emotions function contradictory to our most integral thoughts. Faith with integrity creates an uninhibited lane specifically occupied by the believer.

Faith is developed and restored through withstanding adverse conditions in seemingly less than favorable relationships. Every relationship, intimate, friendship, or career related, will not stand through all the changes of a lifetime. However, it's up to us to decide what, from each of those relationships, we will carry over into the next moment of our lives. We should consciously choose to carry with us only the experiences that will serve to better us in our next relationship. Otherwise doubt has the ability to gain access via unresolved traumatic life experiences

Indecision, is a direct descendent of doubt. It's an extremely dangerous state wherein heightened emotional activity overwhelms our moral compass, hindering its ability to give accurate direction and properly process frustration. It's like pressing the gas pedal of a car while it's in neutral. No matter how much force we exert, because we lack definitive direction (not in gear which says to move forward or backward) we ultimately drift toward the downward sloping places of our life.

Indecision is a result of investing an excessive amount of cognitive capital into volatile emotions. Seeking any form of resolution, we may teeter between seemingly logical and completely irrational thoughts, until the succession of our thoughts has little to no correlation. As our cognitive momentum staggers, our daily physical activities are directly impacted.

In an effort to survive, we begin wildly flailing some of our emotional extremities - pride, ego, sexual misconduct - seeking out sympathy from others, and worst of all complacency. For some, instant gratification becomes the indefinite motivation for living, while others spend their time deliberating but never actually seeking out the purposed desires of their hearts.

Indecision may also arise as a result of witnessed or directly experienced trauma. Trauma may produce triggers that are unknown to others. When people's actions or impulses activate these triggers, mistrust is a prominent response. Mistrust in an extreme form can construct barriers between us and the very opportunities we seek in Love. We should always use discernment in relationship when the actions of others don't align with communicated intentions, as trauma can also leave us doubtful of our ability to make sound decisions. Indecision opposes our will to stand firm in our convictions. In the fight to maintain a sense of control some of us are nearly hysterical, lobbying thoughts void of purpose, holding others accountable for principles we don't follow and making irrational excuses for our actions, or lack thereof.

Without something or someone bringing us back into a place of healthy in relationships, we continue to spiral and ultimately reach a state of all out fear. At this point, nothing has gone the way we expected, and what little hope we have feels forced and unauthentic depending on the moment. We cycle through lows and highs riddled with frustration, doubt and indecision. Our excuses become an ever apparent boomerang coming back to us as a reality check. Something needs to change as fear begins to infect everything of significance in our lives.

Many, including myself, have stayed in uncomfortable but familiar circumstances because of fear and the many prideful excuses that accompany fear. Excuses such as, if I wait a little longer something will change. Still, we can see a need for change, desire better and still refuse to seek it because we're afraid of losing something that is depreciating by the second. Allowing fear to dictate your choices is as sensible as holding your breath for fear of breathing. If air quality is determined by what's emitted into the atmosphere, fear is a pollutant in relationship suffocating possibility. Loving fearfully or Loving from a place of fear significantly decreases the amount of Love you are able to give and receive.

Authentic Love is a filter separating you from your fears and providing fresh experiences for you to breathe in. Like a swaddled newborn baby, some of us will wrap ourselves in the pain of seemingly failed relationships until that solitary state of mind becomes so tight that there is no room to move a single emotional extremity. Some have and will live out the rest of their days suffocating, refusing to breathe, and sabotaging opportunities to Love, while the truth has been and continues to be ever present. There is a huge difference between sufferance and suffocation.

Suffering, in Love, is the way by which we and others come to know the value of our investment and the length to which we must go to attain our desires. Our suffering is a down payment on the legacy we leave for others who will take the journey after us. Suffocation is the deprivation of one's self from the process of our own Love experience by surrendering to fear. We suffocate the possibility and progression of Love for both us and others, leaving a legacy of bitterness.

Approaching every relationship with the same inept strategies from prior experiences, only begets you more of what you've already experienced. If you consciously acknowledge and accept your mistakes and less than desirable proclivities, work to better yourself with a spirit of humility and gratitude, overtime the story you'll write will take the form of the Love you were purposed to live out.

While that relationship may not have ended as either of us desired, I gained insight into what Love requires of us. Patience, kindness, and the value of being open to new experiences are just a few. That experience was a piece, a contribution to my Love story that revealed the struggle to balance my needs and the needs of others in relationship.

Love is not seeking perfection. Love's purpose is to evoke and sustain experiential relationships. It does not hold against us the things we have attempted and seemingly failed at. It patiently attends to our needs, while advocating for the desires of our heart within the universe. It is okay to fall but it's never ok to stay down, especially when Love is the force lifting you back up!

CHAPTER FIVE

LETTING GO

*"The word failure was birthed from humanity's impatience
with life's many processes."*

It wasn't easy letting go of what either of us perceived that that relationship should have been, especially considering the time we had both given to it. Over the span of five years we revisited that relationship on more than one occasion after it initially ended. And while our lives inevitably progressed individually, our ability to progress in Love collectively gradually diminished. Ultimately we agreed that it was best to Love each other from a distance.

Through the years as I've sat with friends or people I've had the pleasure of meeting, I've discovered that far too often we unconsciously invest our time and trust in the very experiences that prohibit us from progressing in life and in Love. We hoard lies that are told to us by others and at times lies we tell ourselves that skew our perspective of reality. We refuse to let go of the unhealthy things done and or said by us and others and instead become the personification of those things. Worst of all we allow the collection of our perceived failures in relationships to be the foundation by which we establish all other relationships, which cripples the possibility of Love growing before it ever takes root. Believing at the essence of all life is Love, I've come to know that Love does not fail. While all experiences may not yield a particularly desired outcome, this does not constitute failure.

I believe the word failure was birthed from humanity's impatience with life's many processes. Consider the Internet as a perfect example of man's impatience. The Internet was operable many years before it ever became available to the general public. Government organizations used the Internet as a way to connect and share information quickly. Eventually the Internet made its way into the homes of global citizens. Initially it was slow, at times unreliable, but we would wait patiently for a dial-up connection. That was likely because the internet was new to the public and it gave us access to things in other parts of the world we had never experienced. We waited for this slow but newly gratifying relationship.

Now the Internet allows us access to everything we want and don't need, whenever we desire. But our ability to be patient, even when it's a matter of milliseconds, is diminishing daily. Numerous times, too many to count, we've each found ourselves complaining about not having service in certain areas. Most often we blame the provider. However, if you don't like the provider of your connection, you can choose another. Today a new provider will even buy you out of your old contract. Captivated by new and exciting advertisements, we may switch providers only to realize the new service is nearly identical to the previous one. Often society's impatience is exploited by those who seek selfish gain and, overtime, substantive connection has diminished even when we have what some would consider the latest and greatest technology.

A dropped signal was not the end of the Internet. The Internet has improved significantly since it was first introduced to the public. No more logging on, today we can simply open an app on our phones or tablets almost anywhere in the world and instantaneously be connected on demand. Seeking a better, not just different, connection is and has always been an area of opportunity. Every day we benefit from the hard work and time spent by those working to improve connectivity. Despite advancements which afford the world access to culture and information in an almost uninhibited way, some again choose to operate in a very selfish and destructive manner.

The Internet analogy is comparable to the discontent many of us experience in our lives and in Love. It's not our failures, but rather our desire and demand for instant gratification that leads to discontentment. Throughout evolution, the word failure and societies associated experiences with perceived failure have developed an increasingly negative connotation. As a result, many of us frivolously use the word failure to cope with our own lack of diligence in the opportunities afforded to us throughout our lives. The very same can be said in Love. If we, by faith, invest our trust in functional relationships that ultimately aligns with our divine truth, at the very least our efforts will yield prospective.

As darkness does give way to light, failure cannot thrive in the mind that has yielded its power of choice to faith in Love and all that it represents in the earth. Failure is a lie in the minds of those who truly believe in Love. Everything is a contribution to our Love story. Each experience is a piece of life's greater purpose helping to shape our lives both individually and collectively.

When we invest our time and energy into doubt, indecision, and fear, these lies not only distract us, but they stand in direct opposition of our divine truth. We invest by way of our expectations. Our expectations are most commonly derived from assumptions formed through a strained relationship with one's own history. Though expectation may not always be accompanied by negative connotation, we often draw from our experiences with past pain to validate doubt, indecision, or fear, rather than dismiss the lies and choosing to focus our time and energy into Love. When we choose to invest in the lies and forgo Love we inhibit healing and forgiveness and remain stagnate in many if not all aspects of our lives.

For some time, divorce, though I've yet to marry, loomed as a black cloud over my head, discouraging my ability to completely believe, much less be inclined, to willingly participate in the institution of marriage. After my parents' marriage ended in divorce, by default I automatically viewed whatever opportunity I had at marriage with a skewed perception. Though I now know this is a lie, many of us unconsciously take similarly traumatic experiences and spread our fears across the spectrum of life. We do so in our careers, educational endeavors, spiritual pursuits, finances and other areas of opportunity. Operating this way will yield a portfolio that consistently trades the currency of life from an emotional deficit.

Throughout my career in human development I've found that we often find ourselves owning the traditions of a past generation without ever truly attempting to objectively examine if they reign true for our self. For many, if not all of us, our dysfunctional or deficient behaviors can be traced back through our individual heritage. My use of the word heritage speaks to our upbringing, the traditions, both consciously and unconsciously, passed down through our lineage.

Personally, it took a great deal of retrospective meditation, focused solely on my own emotional inheritance, to truly get to a place of acceptance regarding my behaviors in relationship and Love. Doing so I was able to see precisely what behaviors I inherited from my mother and what behaviors I inherited from my father. Having gained that perspective, I was then able to make an intelligent decision as to who and how I will be in relationship with life, love and the pursuit of my purpose.

It's vitally important to understand that the parent-child relationship is the most common example wherein we often inherit much of our emotional debt. As a conscious parent, next to physical harm, it is our greatest fear that our children will experience failure in life, Love, or even both. Still so many parents unintentionally and in most cases unconsciously neglect to endow their children with the proper tools and experiences necessary to prepare a child for consistent success in either. Because all parents naturally transfer their life experiences—good, bad or simply tradition—to the next generation, we must also hold ourselves accountable for forwarding on adequate resolution where applicable.

Though I now know divorce is not a generational curse. Many people like me, as a result of inheriting inadequate resolution concerning divorce, have lived and still live not knowing that divorce is not inevitable. Without adequate resolution, divorce and many other variations of painful experiences can become cyclical, one generation to the next, leaving a legacy of hurt that knows no bias.

Now more than ever, it seems we live in a world filled with an overwhelming population of hurt people. The hurt is not geographically specific or biased; it spans age, race, gender, class and every continent. While most are attempting to mask the pain of their past, others fail and fall victim to often unforgiving decisions such as addiction and violence. But then there are also those individuals who are less identifiable. I call them "relational tyrants." "Relational tyrants" are people who ignorantly desire power, position, wealth and the time of others, while simultaneously living a life contradictory to Love's honor system.

Bernard Lawrence "Bernie" Madoff was a relational tyrant. For over 40 years he established relationships with individuals and organizations under the guise of being a trusted advisor. More than four thousand of his clients put heir money in his care, their trust in his words and lost both because Bernie lived a life contradictory to Love's honor system. Love's honor system isn't treating others as you would like to be treated, but rather being concious and caring enough to provide the best of yourself in relationships with others without compromising your integrity. When we are unable to abide by Love's honor system, then it's time to leave the relationship. Unfortunately, relational tyrants don't know when to quit. For years before Mr. Madoff was arrested at his New York home for defrauding his clients of more than $64 billion, he went in to work and perpetuated a lie day after day.

For the addict, there is rehabilitation. Criminals can be sentenced to correction or incarceration. But often times the "relational tyrant" goes on to mercilessly build obstacles where a bridge is necessary, making the progression of life difficult for so many. Some relational tyrants become pastors, political figures, teachers and CEO's. They are decision makers who refuse to choose Love for themselves, yet their decisions or lack thereof negatively impact cities states, and countries in ways that are immeasurable. Adolf Hitler is a perfect example of a charismatic leader without a positive perspective of Love, doing more damage than good. It's fair to say he lacked a keen understanding of compassion and goodwill, the very qualities that a leader should genuinely possess if they are going to make a positive impact anywhere. Because our contributions to the lives of other have a residual effect, the greater our responsibility in relationship to others, the greater our potential impact on their lives.

We all are the sum of our life experiences. No one person or group is solely responsible for all the negative things that happen in life. My true intention is to expose the potential impact of inadequate resolution concerning our experiences that are absent of the Love we need. Within the spectrum of Love, wherever we may be in life, each of us is capable of tremendously impacting the many lives we will encounter spanning our lifetime. This state of consciousness is where authentic Love thrives. Authentic Love is not looking for a party to blame for its seemingly inherent deficient behaviors and or thinking. Nor is it negligent to the fact that they exist. Equipped with the knowledge that the accumulative experiences of humanity make up a life, Authentic Love seeks to sort, store, or let go of each experience adequately. In doing so we more efficiently align ourselves with the purpose of life, which is relationship.

Indefinitely surrendering to any particular traumatic experience will always leave us mentally digging ourselves out of a place authentic Love never physically or psychologically put us in, nor intended for us to be in. This prevents us from the experience of building with the new tools Life and Love have afforded us in the present.

In baseball, a player's bat is the essential key to accessing the path to victory. But once a player hits the ball, whether it's a grand slam home run or a sacrifice bunt, that player must release the bat in order to transition home. Attaining our goals in life and Love are no different. Maybe, there is a particular bat you've swung that's gotten you this far in life. Your looks or your intelligence may have knocked it out of the park up until now but life will at times demand we gain a new perspective. The keys that have opened doors for us before won't always work as we transition to new experiences in life and in Love.

Have you ever attempted to open a door with your hands full? It's difficult and can be absolutely impossible until we're comfortable with letting go of some things. Hoarding the emotional baggage of past life experiences makes it extremely difficult to transition through present moments and other stages of life and Love that will follow. Unresolved negative emotions can constipate relationships and tend to drive a wedge between us and who or what we Love.

It's not easy letting go of people, places, and things that have a played a significant role in our lives. However, if that person, place, or things, is prohibiting us from being fully present in life and Love, it's ok to let go in transition. It's ok to let go of dad's disappointments and the consuming fear that lingers as a result. It's alright to let go of a mother's Love that didn't quite measure up to be exactly what you needed. You should seek out a professional who can help you cope with abuse, molestation, rape, low self-esteem, and depression, without shame. There is no shame in being the best version of you inside and out. Let go of the job that only pays the bills but isn't fulfilling you mentally. The meaningful and well-paying career does exist for you. Mundane relationships that you don't feel valued in are a waste of your time and energy; tap into the Love that is purposed for you. There is more to life and Love than whom or where we have contented ourselves to.

Authentic Love knows and believes in the process of sacrificing its current state or being in the pursuit of divine purpose. Letting go of anything that inhibits us from Loving courageously is required.

CHAPTER SIX

REBUILDING

"The journey to peace doesn't always feel peaceful."

In 1967, the Morris A. Mechanic Theatre, named after a well-known theater operator, was erected in downtown Baltimore to replace the legendary ninety-three-year old Ford's Grand Opera House. Seating just a little over one thousand six hundred patrons during its time of operation, The Mechanic was Baltimore's grand stage for Broadway plays. Although it replaced Ford's Grand Opera House, it had a much shorter reign as Baltimore's top stage for live shows. In 2004, after thirty-three years, the Morris A. Mechanic Theatre closed its doors forever. In 2005, the building was purchased by one developer and another in 2009, only to abandon their plan within that same year.

Almost ten years after its initial purchase after closing, the Mechanic Theatre stood as a shell of its former glory.

On my way to work in downtown Baltimore, I had passed the abandoned building many times, never paying it much attention. I knew of the Mechanic my entire life as just another concrete structure amongst many others. However, in September of 2014, the second developer finally planned for demolition. Fences were erected for safety, assuring that debris and demolition equipment wouldn't come into contact with commuters and pedestrians. The parking garage operating below was closed and soon after demolition began.

I've seen buildings demolished time after time again living in an ever-changing city like Baltimore. As a demolition method, most often those buildings would be filled with strategically placed dynamite or pummeled over and over again using a wrecking ball. In a brief amount of time, the building would come down, and shortly thereafter, a new foundation would be poured for a new structure to take the place of the old.

But I noticed something was different about the demolition of this building. Because of how it was built, it took much longer to demolish. Dynamite was not used in the demolition process, possibly because of its proximity to the public and other important buildings that could not be closed for long periods of time. Therefore, there was no explosive force implemented in the plans of bringing down the old relic, a fitting fate in my eyes.

Once an integral part of Baltimore's cultural identity, the Mechanic was slowly torn down bit by bit as all other life seemingly went on without regard for its legacy. Somehow even in the age of the great electronic distraction, I was unexpectedly captivated by every small bit of progress over the months it took the Morris A. Mechanic Theatre to meet its inevitable fate. I could never have imagined crumbling concrete would facilitate such as reverent experience in me.

It was the meticulous process that convicted me. It reminded me so much of my own life. I couldn't help but consider Love and relationship and the magnanimous structures we build within. The bulky theatre was built in a brutalist style. It was a heavily fortified concrete structure. While brutalist architecture was very popular during the 1950s and up until the 1970s, it didn't fit the modern esthetic of the developing area.

With real effort and energy into relationship, we can become like the fortified concrete of the Mechanic. As we go about our lives, we begin to build in places we believe are purposed. Over time, we erect a variety of monumental relationships with different people places and things. And in the same way the Mechanic met its end, it can appear to take a lifetime to break down the lasting experience that relationship so often is for each of us. Embedded in the many constructs of relationship are joy and pain, hope and expectation, disappointment and self-revelation. We build in anticipation of finding comfort, companionship, understanding and validation. Why would anyone ever want to lose that?

Truthfully, while we all can experience comfort, companionship, understanding or validation in relationship, some don't. For some, it may be because of unresolved traumatic experiences. But others faced with the reality of loss don't have a decision in the matter and are unable to recover from what they perceive as the loss of a great Love. You may be unexpectedly laid off of a job that you've had for years. Or you are at the end of a marriage you've done everything to salvage. Perhaps it is when a Loved one dies: we may find ourselves standing in the rubble of relationship, debris scattered about, with you deciphering what remains in hopes of finding something to retain as proof of significance. What do we do when we've built monumental relationships and we've watched them diminish to the ground level of our lives? We rebuild.

For me nothing in life feels more debilitating then loss of significant relationship. Grieving is an area of opportunity for me. I often know when a specific relationship is headed toward its demise, as most of us do. Still without properly acknowledging this, my faith in relationship can evoke a hope that is ignorant of reality. When a relationship finally ends, I'm at the point of I knew it, but the residual effects of expectation and the absence of present energy requires grieving. When we pretend we're not impacted by loss of significant relationship or try to fill the void of a once present energy with something less substantive, we deprive ourselves of necessary healing. Therefore, I am working everyday to accept the things I'm unable to change. I believe so fervently in the purpose and efficacious impact of healthy relationship for those who are receptive. Reciprocity is essential for a healthy relationship. To facilitate Love reciprocally in healthy relationship with others is my greatest desire and my life's purpose.

I know without loss we would never know the value of the experiences life affords us. In loss, we gain perspective. It's not uncommon for the monumental relationships we've constructed in life to be abandoned -willing or otherwise. Standing alone in the unfulfilled expectation of relationship provides a clarity we may not have noticed before. We may see the things we could have said and done differently. We may hear the voice of compassion and replay the most significant and beautiful moments. Or we may experience a peace we so desperately need.

The journey to peace doesn't always feel peaceful. In fact, it can feel like hell on earth. Still every breath is proof of the purpose of our existence. Some breaths are a little harder to take then others as some moments in life are harder to experience. We all face moments of quiet suffering. Away from the chatter is the perfect time to analyze our portfolio of emotional currency to determine how our investments are faring as our lives progress.

Overtime, we accumulate so many emotional experiences in building relationships, that we can't consciously be aware of every experience in every moment. We have to work to continuously strengthen our consciousness through consistently considering how our decisions impact us and others. Life is not solely about what we create to live out our own purpose. It's also about how what we create contributes to humanity. As we build relationships with those we are directly connected to, we indirectly build relationships with others. They may not know us by name or face, but they do know the residual impact of our contributions made in direct relationship with others.

Like The Mechanic, people come to know us for who we have been. Our words and actions played out overtime create a specific perception. This can make transitioning through life difficult because people expect what they have perceived. They don't always get to witness everything that goes into the construct of relationship. Most specifically, when it comes to the relationships we build with ourselves, others may be completely oblivious to what is going on in the inside.

I'm not sure why the demolition of The Morris A. Mechanic Theatre wasn't one giant explosion. But I imagine, much like with many of us, there were some delicate spots which required a very specific process. There is always a demolition of sorts before rebuilding in Love. The demolition of toxic relationships often requires a purging of emotions, possibly a reconciliation of self with bad decisions and disconnecting yourself from toxic people and thoughts. I remember watching one man working on the demolition site holding a water hose suppressing the spread of dust and debris as the wrecking ball would smash into the fortified concrete.

I thought of my own life experiences. I thought of the people who covered me with Love when the consequences of my decision were wrecking my life. I can't imagine the outcome if the debris from my actions, absent their Love, were to impact the perceptions of others. I'm grateful for the integrity of those individuals that covered me. At the same time let me say that I don't believe that other people's perceptions of us are of the utmost importance. Everyone should not know all of us, some things should be between us and those who genuinely Love us. Many people lack the ability to see us as good and perceive that we are still capable of making unfavorable decisions. No matter how many relationships we construct, experience alone does not make a master builder. Wisdom is developed in our consistent commitment to the integrity of every relationship.

When opportunity enters our lives, briefly or otherwise, a plan for how our time will be spent must be established before we move to do anything. We should stay encouraged also knowing blueprints often take a few drafts before being finalized. It's easy to grow impatient in the drafting process, the periods of planning action but not completely carrying it out just yet. Today, the Morris A.

Mechanic Theatre is no more. After more than ten years since it closed, the site where the theatre stood for thirty-three years is leveled to its foundation. I've passed it almost every week since demolition started in 2014, but now there are no more wrecking balls, no workers; the site sits dormant.

Held up by lawsuits, the plan to construct a two-tower apartment building with retail space is on hold. The Broadway shows have found a new home in Baltimore at The Hippodrome Theatre. I've even been a few times. While a resolution will certainly come at some point, in the meantime, the rest of the city continues to develop around the site where The Mechanic once stood. At times life may feel like that for many of us. We watch others seemingly progressing as our own lives appear to be in a state of dormancy.

Someone I have great respect for once told me, "If you compare your life to others, you will always come up short." When we attempt to establish our Life, our Love story, upon the premise of others, we will always see things with a skewed perception. If we see ourselves as having or being more, we devalue ourselves. If we see ourselves as being or have not quite enough, we devalue ourselves. Even as the site of the former Morris A. Mechanic Theatre sits abandoned, its property value is still increasing simply by the nature of where it is located. Sure, its current owner is losing money in taxes, court fees, and money is not being made because there is no income currently being generated from the site. But the wise investor knows the value of having patience in waiting for better. Over time what we erect, when done with integrity, will turn a direct and residual profit for us if we manage it well.

In the 1960's, there were several buildings built during the time of the Mechanic Theatre. Some of those buildings still stand today, repurposed, renovated; and others are torn down and rebuilt. Life and Love exist in the same way. We are constantly renovating and rebuilding. We must grow to trust the drafting process, adapt to an ever-changing world, and build with integrity. Doing so with Love assures that the things we construct will be meaningful.

People often blame the heart for decisions that breed less than favorable outcomes. But science lets us know that the heart's function is to control the flow of blood throughout our bodies. The heart does not have literal emotions. It does not make decisions absent of the mind. We should acknowledge this truth in our rebuilding process. Our favorable and less than favorable decisions both centrally take place in the mind. Believing the heart somehow overrides the mind leads to misconceptions in Love. The heart does not have wants absent of the mind and should not be used as a scapegoat for poor decision making.

To know that we build from a centralized cognitive operating center helps to more readily define the constructs of our relationships. In essence, we are not feeling or experiencing anything our brains have yet to also perceive.

As we go about establishing ourselves in the world, we are capable of being actively engaged in every experience with the full measure of our being. As we build relationships, we don't have to segregate or compartmentalize any part ourselves.

In our journey to Authentic Love we must require the same from those we choose to build relationship with. Though Love requires for us to be compassionate, compassion can never be actualized at the expense of our integrity. Authentic Love will not honor our lack of integrity for self. Nor will the thing or person we've compromised our integrity for value the sacrifice being made. Authentic Love does not ask of us things that will diminish our character in the presence of others. More importantly, authentic Love does not ask of us things that will negatively impact our thoughts and feelings toward ourselves. Love is always reverent of the human condition. It takes pride in doing well by others and for self.

The time we take to rebuild is spiritual. It's is an assessment of the accumulative perspective we've gained from every relationship we've established. It's the soul's opportunity to restructure our portfolio of emotional capital and reinvest in the things that are good and good for us. Rebuilding is the moment between the exhale and the inhale. We should cherish it knowing that what lies ahead is as great as we believe and as Loving as we chose to be.

CHAPTER SEVEN

INSANITY

"There is beauty in the insanity Love can seemingly produce."

"They say insanity is doing the same thing over and over and expecting a different result." I've heard that so many times in counsel and conversation with people about their relationships. My response is always, "I believe 'they' lack perspective as to what Love authentically is."

Undiscovered mental illness withstanding, making unfavorable decisions with a "present mind" is not insanity; it is bad judgment. And yes, some of us exercise extremely bad judgment, including myself at various points in my life. However, good judgment is developed overtime as is a healthy relationship with Love.

Most of us began our very first relationship the same way we began our life, unlearned and curious. We all make unfavorable decisions. We all experience unfavorable outcomes. There are also those of us whose introductions to relationship are tainted with the unfavorable decisions of others. Nonetheless, be it the unfavorable decisions of our own making or the unfavorable decisions of others, seeking resolution and healing is the only way to truly progress in life and Love. I encourage anyone who has experienced trauma or abuse of any kind to seek the help of a professional because our minds don't heal themselves. It takes conscious effort.

I'm such a fervent believer in resolution because I've experienced relationships in which there was none. Though I've come to know that people can only build with the tools that they have, and additionally know how to properly use, my early assumption was that people simply didn't care enough to do or be better. So I would treat them that way and it was a hindrance to Love.

I had to seek positive resolution because the assumption I made is not always true. Nor should it be our designated mentality in every relationship to assume that people don't care when things don't coincide with our desired outcome. We should work constantly to overcome our fears and consistently seek the truth concerning our assumptions. When we don't, we may find ourselves becoming the personified versions of those very fears and assumptions.

Fear and assumptions corrode our perspective of reality. They produce and increase erratic thoughts and behavior. They foster an environment of unpredictability and the notion that those thoughts and behaviors are justified. Because no relationship can survive such conditions, people who live without resolution typically jump from one relationship to the next, often before the first ends. They generally check out mentally the moment they feel their thoughts and behaviors are unjustly being challenged. It doesn't matter that they are not consistent in either, even when they know it.

Love does not discriminate; it presents each of us with an opportunity to experience relationship. However, the thoughts and actions within the relationship produce its outcome. Over the days, months, and years that chronicle a relationship, it's not the things that we do differently, but rather the things we do and say consistently, especially when faced with adversity, that become the construct and sustenance of our relationships. In pursuit of a genuinely sustainable relationship, we typically choose our partner because of the consistency and diligence that anchor the core of their character. It's impossible to find a successful relationship wherein one or both parties struggle to be consistent in their communicated core values. While being predictable can be boring in some aspects of relationship, we all have a few things that when done consistently in relationship validates our feelings and help to reassure that a certain level of care and understanding is present.

The things we do inconsistently can also become the construct of a relationship. Unaddressed and uncorrected, inconsistent and sporadic behaviors develop into habits. Such habits are adversarial to the stability and progress of any relationship. Sporadic and emotionally charged decisions cause ripples of energy that often negatively affect unintended bystanders with or without our knowing.

If Love is truly what we are seeking, then we must also seek to be a representation of Love consistently. It is easy to identify what you're in search of when what you are looking for is at work inside of yourself. Nothing knows Love more authentically then Love itself. As we mature, relationship becomes less about a particular perception of happiness and more about authentic Love.

While many of us would like to characterize Love in its most honorable state as "unconditional, "I ask whoever on earth has ever seen it? What tangible representation can you offer to authenticate the belief that "unconditional" Love truly does exist? In fact, all Love is conditional. There has not and never will be any form of unconditional Love in the earth.

The closest that human beings have come to unconditional Love is the exchange between an infant and its dedicated parent. Yet even this Love is rooted in conditions. Parents have an innate obligation to nurture and protect their newborn offspring due to the helplessness that is infancy. Though some parents neglect that obligation, others are conditioned to the joy that comes with having created life and the accomplishment one feels knowing your child is well taken care of and progressing. These conditions are both wonderful and consuming. The latter often proves to be the reason why many people choose not to have children. However, beyond the parent child relationship, the conditions of Love are more diverse and increasingly consuming.

As we diligently seek to experience Love authentically in our life experiences we must understand and accept authentic Love as conditional Love. One of the founding conditions of authentic Love is sacrifice. Sacrifice is the down payment we all make to afford the necessary suffering that Love requires. The suffering we experience in sacrifice is the cognitive equivalent of the tension and fatigue our bodies feel when we exercise underutilized muscles. As we tone and shape our relationships, the suffering that we experience is building the foundation and infrastructure necessary to build strength, stamina and flexibility in our relationships.

It's important that we know the difference between pain and suffering. Pain is more of a temporary mental state than a requirement of relationship while suffering, in contrast, through compassion allows us to understand the comprehensive value of Love.

The saying, "You will never know Love until you've known pain," lacks definitive truth. Love can certainly exist without the negative cognition associated with pain. And while pain has value, it is transient and often an unreliable gauge of someone or something's permanence in our lives. Pain often convolutes a present opportunity for understanding and amicability within relationship. What pains you may not cause me pain and vice versa. In labeling pain as a requirement of Love, we unconsciously give permission to ourselves and those who we are in relationship with to measure the value of our Love experiences by the level of pain we experience in them. This system of thought will always fail to balance out. If the scales are weighted by life experiences, socioeconomic status, and an onslaught of exhaustive things that will bring about division rather than reciprocity, relationships become a selfish and never-ending competition about who's experienced the most pain.

Suffering, comparatively, knows pain and endures it when necessary, with the knowledge that its cause is greater than one's self. Suffering is best identified in the fatigued hours we spend in search of bettering our performance at work or developing our own business. Suffering is the discomfort experienced and worked through in family counseling or one on one therapy sessions. In the changes or corrections that we make to habits that don't serve the greater calling of our purpose in life and relationship, we will experience suffering. Each sacrifice we commit to for the sake of compassion will unveil authentic Love to us in greater ways than we knew before.

Though sacrifice is the key that opens the door of opportunity, what lies behind the door is choice. In relationships, our choices can be motivated by selfish desires or greater prosperity. If we are building a foundation and infrastructure of authentic Love, every choice must be rooted in selflessness, even if presently the only benefactor is one's self. For example, buying a house may be of benefit to your relationship with yourself. In the process of saving for that purchase, there are often fiscal habits that must be sacrificed to achieve the goal of purchasing a home. As we anticipate future success, we should only expect to see in actuality the things that we have put effort into today. Our past is a reflection of our present, and our present is projection of our future.

Subsequently, we will inherit what is yielded by our choices. However, there is also greater thoughtfulness, beyond our control, continuously contributing to our life in service of every moment we live. In return, we should aspire to contribute something positively by way of our choices that will serve something greater than ourselves. In our intimate relationships with a partner, on our job, or especially in the moments when sacrifice is the last choice we want to make, there is honor in choosing selflessness. Doing so creates a space for what we give to live more freely in the earth and increases the possibility for us to experience what we give reciprocally in life and Love.

Selflessness is not only for the benefit of others. Selflessness is also choosing to righteously protect one's own purpose in the earth and rejecting the desire to participate in relationships that contradict that purpose. Sometimes we selfishly tolerate things we should not under the belief that we deserve the pain we may experience for past decisions. But abuse in any form should never be tolerated under any circumstance. There is never justification for taking advantage of another's Love. Intimate relationship shouldn't lack adequate recognition and appreciation of our efforts to be Loving, employers should not disregard the dedication of its employees, nor should a church the time of its congregation. Relationship is a space for reverence, compassion, growth and understanding. Without these pillars of sustainability, Love is fading or totally absent. Pride is swelling and energy is being mismanaged.

Owning one's energy is the next founding condition of authentic Love. Each choice that we make creates and impacts present energy. We may spend so much time preparing for the future that we forget to live in the present. There is power in being consciously aware of our present and knowing that our future is only a reflection of our thoughts and actions today. What we do right now will be our future. If we Love today as we wish to Love forever, our future will only be a projection of where we are in this very moment. This is why owning one's energy is so vitally important to our Love experience.

In properly owning our energy, we understand that in Love everything cannot receive energy equally. We have to discern and designate what energy will be given, gifted, and exhausted on what, when, and how as well as to what person, place, thing or idea.

Relationships are like maintaining a garden; you intentionally plant what you want to grow. With meticulous care for each seed, a pattern of consistency is developed in an effort to give adequate care to the entire garden. We maintain patience as a virtue in order to see the fruits of our labor. The most intrinsic part of gardening to me is knowing that though all things won't grow in every season, when it is time, each form of whatever you plant will appear as it is purposed. Overtime we learn to abide by the naturally occurring life cycle of creation. Then our gardens flourish, season by season and year after year.

We must be conscious also not to over or under water the seeds we have planted, as balance is essential to a healthy garden. Knowing what emotions and behaviors demand more attention than others, and which desire less, is important for growth. Acting not out of our own feelings toward a thing but rather acting on learned caring behaviors that will nurture a desired outcome allows our relationships to flourish in the same way as would a properly manicured garden. This takes a great deal of willingness.

The willingness to actively participate in healthy relationship is the fourth and final founding condition of Love, and without it the others -sacrifice, choice and owning our energy- are impossible to maintain. The willingness to participate in healthy relationship is also the most difficult of the conditions to practice because as a society we are often taught to remove ourselves from places that are uncomfortable to us. The thought sometimes persist that somewhere out there is a dream job, dream partner or a spiritual experience void of the messiness that being human entails. But that place doesn't exist and isn't meant to.

On the contrary, I've learned that it's most often in places of discomfort that we find our true capacity. With billions of people populating the earth and growing every day, the effects of the messiness produced by the existence of human beings will be present in every experience. But also present will be the beauty of everything that being human entails.

There is beauty in the insanity Love can seemingly produce. There is validation in overcoming tragedy. There is wisdom in suffering. There is life in Love. All are there for us to experience or be skeptical of at times, for us to contribute and or mess up. But most importantly, insanity exists for us to make life better: better than it was before us and better for those who will come after. In our attempts to righteously segregate ourselves from the discomfort of things we don't fully understand, we often become unaware of whom we are. Solitarily confined by our perception only, we are unable to the see the reflection of our thoughts and actions in the impact that we have on others. We must not forget that all of our origins are derived from a common biological thread that makes us more alike than we are different, both in life and in Love.

The value of authentic Love is immeasurable. It is not adversarial or meant to be compared, in an effort to validate our pain or pride. The presence of Love is diminished where pride exists within relationships. Love thrives best in relationships motivated by resolution, while pride stubbornly seeks self-preservation before all other things. In attempting to assert a definitive valuation of Love, Love can be lost to menial things in any moment believed to be worth more to our pride. But truly there is nothing in this world of higher value than authentic Love. To compare Love to anything else is to diminish the value of one's own life. Through sacrificing pride for Love, we build upon meaningful opportunities life affords and inherently increases the value of our lives and the lives of those with whom we are in relationship.

Love does not seek to oppress; neither should we in our ambition to be actively involved in a Loving relationship. A willingness to participate in a healthy relationship means that we accept that righteousness lies in our ability to see imperfections as meaningful. Regardless of our experiences, we need to treat everything as something valuable to be learned from, never seeing ourselves as more or less than but rather different.

We only fail when we will not selflessly give all that we have to contribute in service to a relationship that is greater than ourselves. Insanity lies in holding back our contribution for a greater moment, giving up before exhausting the necessary resources, thinking that we are somehow better than our relationships when we are contributing less than what's required, or if we are inconsistent in our contribution.

We should certainly operate with reason, giving all things adequate and appropriate energy, but to want more without giving your best is an insult to Love.

CHAPTER EIGHT

REVELATION

"i am Love!"

In conversation while sitting in a restaurant in Baltimore, I was asked what Love is to me. I began, "Love is the room we are in, the chairs, the tables, and the inspiration to create it all. It is the air we breathe and every interaction, brief or sustained, over a period of time that we have with every form of life and what each life creates to progress humanity, consciously, and unconsciously." When I finished, it was apparent the individual who asked the question certainly didn't expect my answer. I believe in part because life affords us the opportunity to establish our own perspective of Love through the individual journey we each embark on everyday of our lives.

Let me explain. In 2012, my journey had come to a precipice. I had recently ended a five-year relationship with the young lady from college. As I shared previously, it was the first in which I had made a conscience commitment to Love. In the inception of that relationship, I had no clue what that commitment meant. In the end, my ignorance proved to be my own undoing. I was thoroughly exhausted. I was a first-time father of a two-year-old boy. I was jobless. And I couldn't help but wonder how the hell did I get here? Nothing was as I expected. Everything was the opposite of what I had planned.

Up until that moment, I'd spent the larger part of my life in service to others. At the age of twelve, I began speaking professionally as a youth advocate, empowering my peers and consulting with youth-based organizations to establish best practices. As I grew, so did the work, the audiences and the responsibility. But at twenty-four years old, it all came to a halt, ultimately due to a collective of unfavorable decisions. As I searched for meaning to it all, I came to realize that my commitment to Love lacked actual consciousness. All the blame I wanted to place on others landed on me like an anvil in a Warner Brothers cartoon. It was two tons of truth.

With no other sensible choice, I spent the next two years rebuilding myself. I analyzed every known experience I could recall and consistently challenged myself to make adjustments. I read, I prayed, and I meditated to foster healthy experiences upon which I could continue to build upon. Most importantly, I recommitted myself to Love, with the understanding that Love's presence in my life is not contingent upon personal accomplishments. I willingly surrendered to Love's process.

I had to be still enough to recognize the things that were transpiring around me, the things that I was present for but had no control over. I had to accept the truth about the positive and negative impact of my contributions in relationships. I sought to understand where Love was inadvertently exchanged for selfish desire. As I surrendered, the purpose of my life became clearer and Love's presence became more evident. My developing consciousness made me aware of so much that I desired to share with others on their own journey to Love. My experiences with Love have led me to you.

As the greatest declared minds in history have sought out meaning to the various facets of life, they were all driven by a force, a desire to understand life with greater perspective. As their findings have been shared with the world, others have come along and built upon their works. Thus, purpose begets greater purpose. In our journey to Love every relationship builds upon our Love story.

Love is the sustenance of creation. Some things are created out of need, some are created out of convenience, and others conviction. Regardless, Love is the motivating force giving breath to new life and expanding our consciousness. We experience this progression through relationship. We are not only in relationship with others, but we are in relationship with all things involved in our accumulative life experiences. Our will to seek purpose in life further produces Love for us to share and experience.

The experiences we encounter in Love have immeasurable value, unlike the worth of something contingent upon a monetary figure. Inanimate or non-living things may apreciate in monetary value,withstanding defacement or destruction; in the latter, all value may be loss forever. Comparatively, we as human beings are never journeying backwards. Even when faced with opposition, in our determination to succeed, the journey through propels us to our destiny. We meet our purpose when and where we are intended to throughout the progression of our lives.

Still we often desire an explanation for our misery. Living in a world where many struggle with the coexistence of rape and religion, we question the meaning of life. We witness "good" and "evil" juxtaposed on the same earth, neither seemingly having the upper hand. I've seen this dichotomy unfold before my eyes daily growing up in Baltimore, Maryland where resources, crime and access to education vary drastically in neighboring communities that share the same zip code. One community thrives as the other perishes. I've experienced both plight and prosperity as I've traveled the country in conversation and counsel as a human development consultant.

Consistently engaging in relationship for the purpose of progressing humanity has taught me that though authentic Love exists infinitely, our ability to ignorantly act in opposition of Love exists as well. This act is also known by many as freewill. Freewill, or the ability to choose, is a necessary component of humanity's collective Love experience. Choice, in its intended purpose, validates the authenticity of relationship. It is an unspoken consent agreement with life.

Our comprehension of consent is essential to humanity's evolution and our collective Love experience. Consent when violated by others fosters unauthorized and unjustifiable energy in the lives of those who have been violated. In additions, recklessly abandoning one's own consent facilitates the opportunity for any present energy to impact our lives, even beyond our initial intent. When our actions inhibit choice, we disrupt the consent necessary to validate the authenticity of relationship. We steal from ourselves and others the ability to experience life and Love as it is purposed to us all.

Our thoughts are relative to our life experiences and the experiences afforded to us by way of relationship. As a result, our choices are complex and riddled with subconscious urges and desires, some we don't understand. Nonetheless, every choice is creating a present energy. Because there are so many people, so many experiences, and so many choices, it is impossible to quantifiably measure the impact of them all with absolute certainty. However, as we become more aware of the impact of known experiences, our conscience develops and we are capable of choice that does not obstruct the journey of others. With a developed consciousness, we are able to actively manage the energy produced as a result of our choices.

Mismanaged energy evokes fear. Fear is not of Love. It is an evolutionary response to consciousness. However, Love is ever present, waiting for us to once again come to a place of acknowledgement. Our ability to acknowledge present Love drives out fear, as they cannot occupy the same space simultaneously.

Love does not demand its own way. It has no desire to be pursued in fear or obstructed by complacency. It is the currency of the courageous. Love is the coherent will to give the better part of oneself to a person or cause, incorruptibly enduring all things, with the faith that every contribution is serving the greater good of that person or cause. As we surrender to Love, inherently we welcome it more freely into our lives. Our collective contributions facilitate a greater shared Love experience. The greater our experience, the more conscious our choices are concerning Love. More conscious decisions yield an energy that evokes favorable outcomes for us and all life entirely.

The origin of life is arguably the greatest debate of man's existence. However, in my household that debate was pretty one-sided from birth until adulthood. My parents are both Baptist ministers. Though neither was overtly religious, I spent what felt like the entirety of my childhood within the walls of church, except when I was in school. After my parents divorced and we left the church we were attending, I wasn't made to go church as frequently. And when I became of age to make my own decisions concerning church, naturally, I rebelled.

I was anxious to explore the world outside of the perimeters of religion. My ideas of life, even in my youth, didn't always fit into the box of religious tradition. I was an opinionated child with a propensity to speak my mind absent of considerable thought for where I was. As I matured, I quickly realized my rebellion continuously put me face to face with many principles, absent of religious tradition, that were ironically similar to the biblical principles I'd learned growing up in church. These principles encouraged humanity to be responsible and caring in our shared experience with others. Many other religions and spiritual practices had these common principles as well. They also existed in the value system of some atheists, agnostics, and undeclared.

Though our beliefs concerning the origin of life and the value placed on particular principles differ, we are all still connected by virtue of one common experience: relationship. It's undeniable that relationship is an essential part of life. It was because of relationship, at twenty-four years old, I found myself right back where it all began. I'd wake up every morning, pray, and then read a scripture before starting my day. It wasn't church, but the principles were still present.

My morning routine was less about religion and more about relationship. More particularly, the one I was building with myself. One particular morning, I came across a scripture, 1 John 4:8. It says, "Whoever does not Love does not know God, for God is Love." And then it hit me... God is Love. I had heard it a thousand times before. I'd even read it before, but that day it grabbed me with a familiar understanding. What accompanied that understanding was a revelation.

"i am Love."

I am an extension of God consciousness, communing with God through relationship, by way of the ultimate shared experience called life. We are an extension of God's consciousness, experiencing God as we commune with one another through relationship by way of the ultimate experience called life. Love has afforded us this opportunity, as it is the sustenance of creation.

Though some would deny that there is a force sustaining life, experiencing creation through relationship, and transacting in the currency of inspired conciseness, I encourage them to take a look in the mirror for proof. We are living, breathing proof of creation, as we ourselves create and reproduce offspring, offspring who also have the ability to do the same. It is by conscience design that we are Love personified, perpetually evolving to greater consciousness.

Science is an integral part of understanding the evolution of life and the progressive consciousness of creation. One does not exist separate of the other. The composition of life is both biological and spiritual, forming physical and psychological bonds by nature of relationship. Those who deny evolution and those who deny creation both stand in contradiction to Love.

Undeniably there are many mysteries of life for which there appear to be no explanation. These mysteries exist, not because of a lack of evidence, but rather due to inadequate understanding of life at a particular stage in our evolutionary journey. Throughout history, man has often associated value to what we believe in, and disregarded those things that challenge our perception. Inspired by hope, the ambitious faith of a few, who sought understanding, garnered contributions of immeasurable value. Those contributions are some of evolution's greatest perpetuators of evolving consciousness of humanity.

Love willingly facilitates the opportunity for humanity's continued evolution beyond every moment in life that our perceptions stagnates our will to seek a greater consciousness. Our hopeful participation in a collaborative consciousness greater than our selves consummates the purpose of our existence. Our various origins, cultures, traditions, and beliefs are allies in our participation of collaborative consciousness. Everything is a contribution to our Love story.

We have experienced Love's presence, in the moments that inspire us to willingly give in service to something greater than ourselves. We have experienced the absence of Love in acts that violate consent and inhibit conscience choice. We are coauthors of our story, with a great responsibility to make substantive contributions to progress the evolution of ourselves and others. Every day we live, is proof of our purposed existence. It validates our ability to overcome the things that stagnate our process and affords each of us the opportunity to both experience and create things that influence humanity's greater consciousness.

As we are Love, anything we do absent of our authentic self inhibits us from experiencing our purposed existence. When we are fully present in our being of Love, we are transformative, we are capable of healing broken places, inspiring acts of courageousness and inciting hopefulness. At our best, Love is like breathing, we are as air to relationship, proof of collaborative consciousness. We are one and the sum of our experiences. We are Love!

CHAPTER NINE

FREEDOM

"The audacity of Love defies logic."

There's a former slave plantation in Towson, Maryland where I go sometimes, often just to be still. Today it's known as Hampton National Historic Site. I go there in part to admire the beautiful landscape. Ironically not too long ago, its grounds were being maintained by individuals who are ex-offenders participating in a re-entry program. At one point Hampton was the largest private home in the U.S., owned by the Carnan-Ridgely family. The estate at its peak was about twenty-five thousand acres. It's recorded that at one point the Carnan-Ridgley family owned about 311 slaves between their collective properties.

While there are physical representations of what life was like during the time of slavery in America, there is also a relentless allure to what is absent. Void of oppression, a place that once was a symbol of injustice and inequality, is now an opportunity to experience peace and the beauty of life uninhibited by man's follies. This place for me represents more than I can intellectually put into words. It's a spiritual experience that at times can be pleasantly overwhelming. It was there that I actualized one of Love's greatest truths: Freedom.

For years I wondered how I could experience so much pain in relationship while motivated by "good and righteous" intention. I labored over the thought questioning how can the Love I give and profess be so gravely misunderstood and produce such unimaginable misery, each time seemingly a greater failure than before. I believed that I had been a good person, a good partner, an exemplary employee. I have always done my best to treat everyone well. Yet, still at times I've found myself hurt and confused, in spite of my best efforts.

Admittedly, I was easily offended in relationship when things were not going the way I expected or planned. I had put a lot of thought and energy into analyzing things time and time again, attempting to find resolution for what I believed was inhibiting my Love experience. My focus was more on the things everyone else was doing rather than taking a healthy assessment of my own actions. Then I chose to be honest with myself about the traits and tendencies I have accumulated over the years. Considering me the constant amongst the variables of life, internalizing my inquiries provided the opportunity to better determine what I was contributing to such unfortunate outcomes. My initial confrontation with myself exposed me to how dangerous a place the mind is if you are not fond of honesty. Honest self-reflection is intimidating and unapologetic.

Lies and excuses are often the catalyst of fictional liberation for those who neglect responsibility for their undesirable actions or unresolved life experiences. But in the posture of honest self-reflection, as quickly as you're able to make up an excuse for poor decisions, your conscience is there to hold you accountable for all feeble attempts at justification. In honest self-reflection, lies are as rotting trash, disrupting the potential for inner peace. Regardless of what you do to mask the odor only complete removal will eliminate the lingering affect and or effects of deteriorative lies.

In my desire for authentic resolution, I spent time obsessing over essential and non-essential relationships, specifically analyzing the potential impact of the contributions I've made over the years. My search revealed to me what I believe is essential in understanding freedom specifically where Love is concerned.

Our subconscious mind is not as easily freed as our conscious mind. As it naturally functions, the unconscious mind stores unknown amounts of information, gathered from the experiences of our life. We draw from this well of information at a time our natural defenses deem necessary. Inadvertently, this may cause us to react to something in our newly found freedom, the same way we would have in captivity.

For example, an employee who transitions from United Parcel Services or UPS to work for Federal Express, also known as FedEx, would be foolish to arrive to his new place of employment dressed head to toe in all brown. There is nothing that brown can do for you there. While certainly foolish, that analogy is similar to how we can show up in a new relationship wearing the same pain, anger, expectation, and lack of resolution from unfavorable experiences before, thinking that we've freed ourselves while our minds still live in captivity. I use the term captivity in a metaphoric sense, understanding that captivity often produces two psychological postures.

The first is complacency. Complacency is a taught or adopted practice. It is not a naturally occurring position in life, especially when our sense of comfort is compromised. However, many of us have built such an immense tolerance for complacency that we exist in a semi-conscious state of being. Complacency, uninterrupted, subsequently produces a spirit of entitlement. With time, we begin to feel that we deserve to be where we are. Even if we desire change, complacency will hinder our efforts to see actual change in our lives.

Complacency often enters our lives unnoticed, and typically sustains itself by thriving on the fears we refuse to find resolution for. We see the effects of complacency daily. At our jobs people may complain about what's wrong but do nothing to fix it. We see the effects of complacency in our homes when we avoid tough conversation and true resolution, while families fall apart. We've all heard of religious and other not-for-profit organizations that collect funds for buildings that are never erected and causes that never receive the aid promised. Still we tolerate and even follow the ways of other human beings with tainted experiences and minimal competency, as we completely isolate those who are desperately in need, those who care, and those who deserve better than our complacent selves.

In being complacent, we often reserve ourselves to a disposition of hindrance in relationship for fear of loss. This may cause unintended damage in the lives of those who are present to progress our purpose at a particular time. Even in wanting to "do no harm," we can cause more damage than good. Good intentions and self-proclaimed righteousness are worthless where complacency abides.

The second psychological posture captivity produces is segregation, the act of setting something or someone apart from other things and/or people. In all of us exists unconscious similarities wired into our thought processes. Love and the desire to know Love's presence is the most common. We are all born of similar biological compositions, we share common traits and emotions, still many of us spend so much of our existence trying our best to set ourselves apart from the other billions of people inhabiting planet earth. Segregation by race, color, class, gender, and a few I've not mentioned, has stained the history of man's existence.

A similar stain taints many of our relationships. We segregate ourselves in fear of what we don't understand. We segregate ourselves when we lack hope. We segregate ourselves when things are tougher than we expect. But nothing segregates us more than when we are guilty of living in opposition of the things or peoples that serve our greater purpose.

It's often a semi-conscious segregation that pits us against the things and people we Love and that Love us. In relationships when we know that there is an ever present and increasing distance, it's not ok to allow the relationship to just drift apart. To give nothing is to receive nothing in return, because what we contribute to our relationships will exist more freely within them. If you have not considered and contributed to your assignment in relationship to the degree which you are asked, required or at least capable of, then you are the problem in your own life. Showing up does not guarantee success or acknowledgement. Showing up, simply places you in the arena. Showing up consistently may provoke opportunity. However, when opportunity comes, you must determine if you are a gladiator, giving everything you are capable of for freedom, or a spectator, merely watching and speaking to things others do.

If our best choice is to terminate the relationship, both parties benefit from adequate closure. All relationships may not last forever, but the effects of relationships are forever changing the lives of all parties involved. Segregation is the abandonment of principles and ethics. If a relationship's principles are abandoned, Love cannot thrive. To abandon another in Love is to recklessly cause a pain in the world for others to experience. This promotes fear, captivity of the mind and an energy inhibiting humanity from Loving more freely.

I often go back to sit and think about what life must have been like for those 311 men, women, and children at Hampton in Maryland. I can only imagine what kind of will it took for them to survive. I imagine the faith they had in spite of their circumstances. Yet what inspires me most is to imagine the Love that persisted while enduring the suffering of captivity. The audacity of Love defies Logic. It hurdles obstacles in pursuit of purpose and emancipates self and others in the process.

As I've journeyed to freedom in my own Love story, there are three specific truths I've identified concerning freedom in Love. The first is that freedom comes at an immeasurable cost. The journey is exhausting and seemingly unforgiving. It can be an ugly endeavor and often the urge to quit will taunt you incessantly. But quitting will surely be the death of the progress you seek.

Second, at times the pursuit of freedom can feel so oppressive it may inspire a longing for the pain of the very captivity we may be in escape of. But turning back can create future chains of bondage. Establishing new ties with old issues gives them relevance in a newly accessed part of your life they don't understand, therefore certainly cannot appreciate. This automatically devalues our progress and stagnates momentum.

Third, being free from something does not ensure relief of its existence in our minds. Freedom grows nearer in our daily pursuit of it. With each step, we are able to bear witness to what we so fervently sought after. Our pain and efforts are never without reward. Yet, after we've attained physical freedom, we have to work daily to pursue liberation of our minds.

Authentic Love exists for the sake of cultivating freedom of the spirit by way of the mind and body. The body is the physical presence of the spirit and the mind as the interpreter of every interaction. As we interact with life outside of ourselves, we find purpose in the things we Love and we find conflict in that which we have yet to understand. In every interaction, authentic Love is compassionate to the conditions of the human experience.

In its desire to be understood, Love is cautious not to harm others.

Our freedom, both collectively and individually, is contingent upon the presence of authentic Love in our life and in every relationship with which we associate ourselves. Relationship is not about absolute mutual benefit. Life does not dictate absolute mutual needs to all of humanity, therefore, benefits also vary. Relationship does, however, facilitate the possibility for all needs to be met when the parties involved are selflessly committed to the communicated and common goal of Love.

Love in relationship is tough at times. It is exhausting and demands that we often see the people and things we Love most at their worst. The reward however, is that we ultimately experience the best of life when we endure with faith and compassion. Life and Love do not exist without adverse experiences. But adversity met with relentless courage is the opportunity for us to rewrite our Love story. When we lack courage, we inhibit progress.

Imagine if the brave souls who fought and journeyed to freedom before us lacked courage. What if not one single person defied the odds? And though the stories we may identify with vary, be it an ancestor who migrated, or a first-generation college graduate, or someone overcoming mental health issues, we all possess the potential to access ancestral courage.

If my mother would have lacked the courage to pursue her entrepreneurial endeavors, I may not have known that Love for myself. If my dad would have lacked courage in his pursuit of God, I may never have known that Love for myself. The decisions they made were not easy and at times defied logic. Still they persisted for a Love that continues to free them and others.

This book is more than the words written on its pages, more than the thoughts assembled and bound between its covers. The experiences I've been afforded and now share with you, is Love given to me, that I give to you, in hope that you may experience freedom in Love. As a result, I hope that you would seek to court purpose in life by seeking Love first in every relationship. I hope that your decisions regarding everything would be rooted in authentic Love only. I hope that as you are moving in whatever direction you choose that you would be conscious of what you bring, while using considerable thought in the handling of others. Know that if you happen to fall, Love is and always will be the force lifting you back up to meet your purpose.

We let go, not to forget, but to access new levels of Love we have yet to experience as we rebuild. We must accept and adapt to loss, understanding that it is the only way we truly know the value of the things life affords us. We are not insane to choose Love, in fact we are courageous. Love defies logic yet is still functional. It is perpetually working to free us from our adverse experiences and expand our consciousness of our intended purpose in the earth.

In Love, there is infinite possibility. When that possibility meets the opportunity that relationship affords us, we are able to experience freedom, Love without limits.

If I could speak all the languages of earth and of angels, but didn't love others, I would only be a noisy gong or a clanging cymbal. [2] If I had the gift of prophecy, and if I understood all of God's secret plans and possessed all knowledge, and if I had such faith that I could move mountains, but didn't love others, I would be nothing. [3] If I gave everything I have to the poor and even sacrificed my body, I could boast about it; but if I didn't love others, I would have gained nothing.

[4] Love is patient and kind. Love is not jealous or boastful or proud [5] or rude. It does not demand its own way. It is not irritable, and it keeps no record of being wronged. [6] It does not rejoice about injustice but rejoices whenever the truth wins out. [7] Love never gives up, never loses faith, is always hopeful, and endures through every circumstance.

[8] Prophecy and speaking in unknown languages and special knowledge will become useless. But love will last forever! [9] Now our knowledge is partial and incomplete, and even the gift of prophecy reveals only part of the whole picture! [10] But when the time of perfection comes, these partial things will become useless.

[11] When I was a child, I spoke and thought and reasoned as a child. But when I grew up, I put away childish things. [12] Now we see things imperfectly, like puzzling reflections in a mirror, but then we will see everything with perfect clarity. All that I know now is partial and incomplete, but then I will know everything completely, just as God now knows me completely.

[13] Three things will last forever—faith, hope, and love—and the greatest of these is love.

The Bible, New Living Translation

ACKNOWLEDGEMENTS

I am eternally grateful for the relationships that inspired *i am Love.* Every experience that led to this moment has certainly not be perfect, but every piece has certainly been a contribution.

With that said:

Mom, I did it! You can cross this off of the list of things I have to do before you die. I'm still working on the singing piece, but I'll make it happen. Dad, thank you for every talk and every lesson you've shared in hopes that I would make better decisions. Thank you both for instilling in me a passion to selflessly serve others. For years I've watched you dedicate countless hours to bettering the lives of every one you meet and it continues to motivate me to do the same.

Kyle, thanks for always supporting me and encouraging me to be a better man and father. Joseph, I'm very proud of you and I look forward to watching you grow and become a great Green man. Ari, I pray that the example I set is a foundation for you to have unconstrained access to your purpose and prosperity. You are my greatest blessing.

Mike, you are one of the best men I know - certainly top three, an amazing dad and though not by blood, I consider you my brother. Alonna, you keep me sane. Kim, you Love me without judgment. Brooke, you inspire me to be relentlessly courageous. Fantastic Fran, the world knows there's only one! Thank you all for everything! The friendships I share with you are invaluable. Thank you for fostering an uninhibited space to be wrong, to heal and to grow.

Ryan and Taryn thank you for covering me in prayer. Thank you for believing in me and thank you for sowing into my life and the lives of others immeasurably. David thank you for pushing me to set and meet my deadline for *i am Love*. You and Lamar took on a twelve year old kid, with a chip on his shoulder, and taught me about being a man who Loves his work, his life and his family.

Faye Wilson, Ed.D. thank you for the time you spent editing and conversing with me to complete *i am Love.*

To those I've not mentioned: it would take another book to thank you all individually. Please know that my life overflows with appreciation for everything that you are to me!

I Love you all!

ABOUT THE AUTHOR

JAMES E. GREEN JR., is a professional speaker and relationship strategist. For more than 15 years his aptitude and passion for relationship building has helped people across the United States strategically develop healthy relationships with self and others through evoking a consciousness to *Love*. His expertise and compassion for the human condition has since become an impetus for progress in the lives James has touched through partnerships with school systems, correctional institutions, corporate entities, non-profits, religious organizations and various municipalities across the country. Through honest self-reflection, shared life experiences and insightful teachings about the transformative power of *Love,* James continues to solidify his position as a dynamic innovator in the world of human development.

JEGREEN365.com
Facebook.com/Jegreen365
Twitter: @Jegreen365
Instagram: @Jegreen365

Made in the USA
Columbia, SC
08 October 2017